JONATHAN DOVE

Te Deum

for SATB Choir and Organ

PETERS EDITION LTD

A member of the EDITION PETERS GROUP
LEIPZIG · LONDON · NEW YORK

Scoring

SATB Choir
Organ

Duration: 6.5 mins approx.

Commissioned by Merton College, Oxford as part of the Merton Choirbook, *a collection of music assembled to celebrate Merton College's 750th anniversary in 2014.*

First performed on 14 September 2014 by the Choir of Merton College, conducted by Benjamin Nicholas.

This score reflects the state of editorial work and correction as at May 2014.

Te Deum

Jonathan Dove

Edition Peters 72592

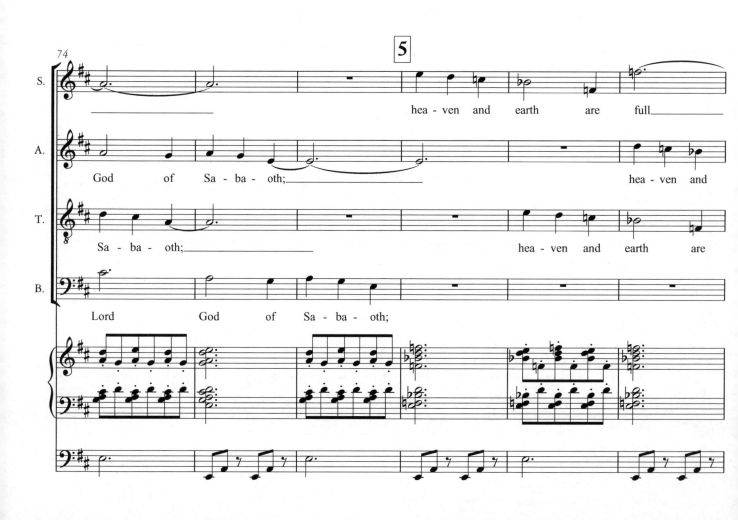

*fragments of words in [square brackets] are not to be sung: they indicate the vowel to be prolonged.

The good - ly fe[llowship]*_____

The good - ly fel - low - ship_____

The good - ly fe[llowship]*_____

The good - ly fel - low - ship_____

The good - ly fe[llowship]*_____

The good - ly fel - low - ship_____

The good - ly fe[llowship]*_____

The good - ly fel - low - ship_____

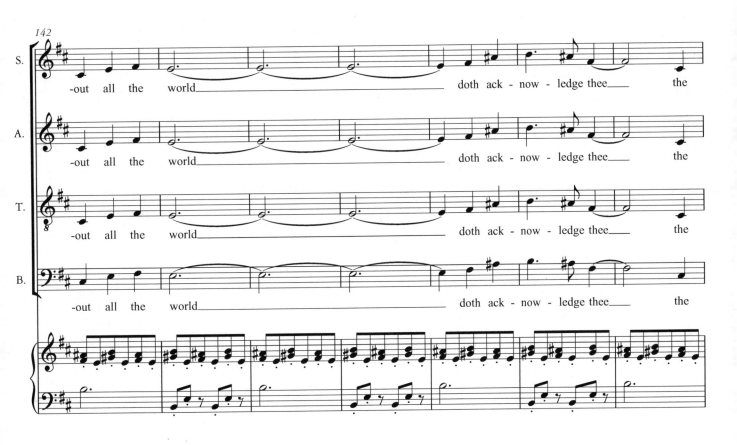

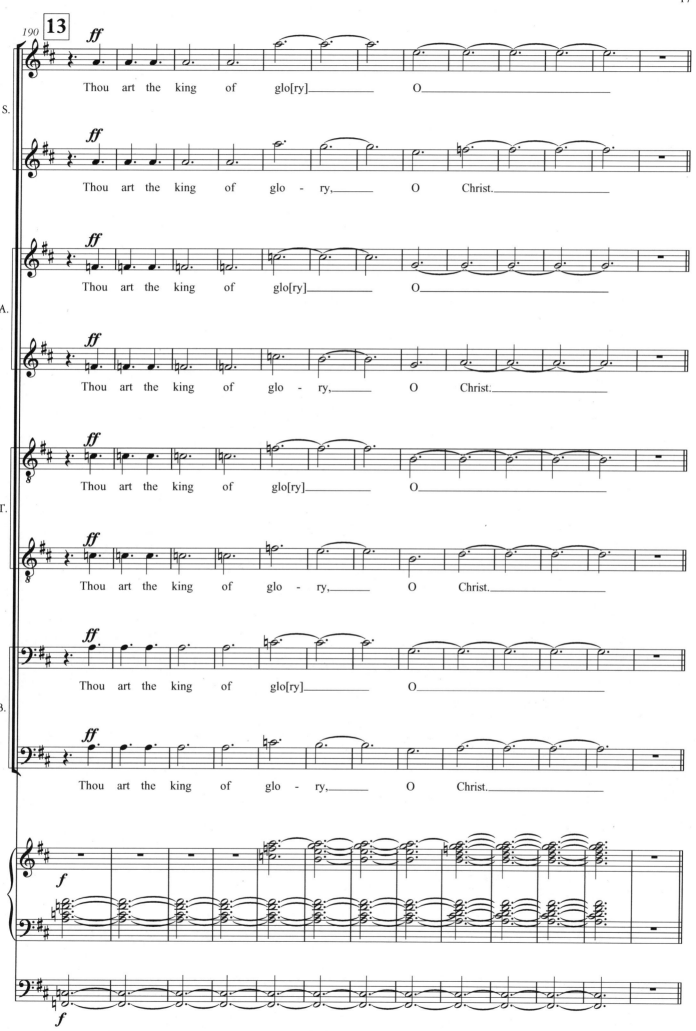

14

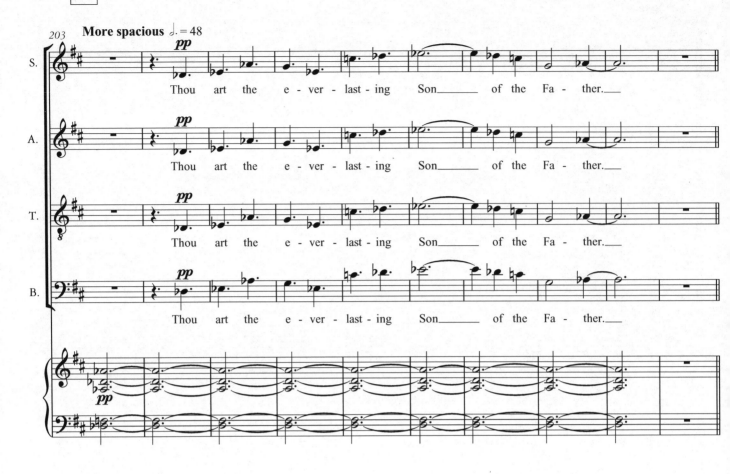

15

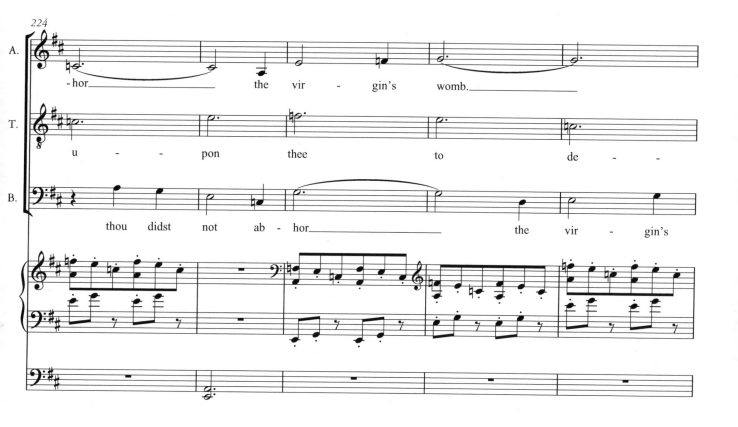

* see note p. 9

25

32